BOSTON RED SOX

ALL-TIME GREATS

BY TED COLEMAN

Book design by Jake Slavik
Cover design by Jake Slavik

Photographs ©: Nick Wass/AP Images, cover (top), 1 (top); AP Images, cover (bottom), 1 (bottom), 4, 7, 12, 14; Ted Sande/AP Images, 8; Harry Cabluck/AP Images, 10; Larry Goren/ Four Seam Images/AP Images, 16; Tom DiPace/PACET/AP Images, 18; Kathy Willens/AP Images, 20

Press Box Books, an imprint of Press Room Editions.

ISBN
978-1-63494-501-1 (library bound)
978-1-63494-527-1 (paperback)
978-1-63494-577-6 (epub)
978-1-63494-553-0 (hosted ebook)

Library of Congress Control Number: 2022902478

Distributed by North Star Editions, Inc.
2297 Waters Drive
Mendota Heights, MN 55120
www.northstareditions.com

Printed in the United States of America
082022

ABOUT THE AUTHOR

Ted Coleman is a freelance sportswriter and children's book author who lives in Louisville, Kentucky, with his trusty Affenpinscher, Chloe.

TABLE OF CONTENTS

SPEAKER
2

CHAPTER 1
THE GOLDEN ERA

The Boston Red Sox played their first season in 1901. Back then, they were known as the Boston Americans. Pitcher **Cy Young** was a key member of the team. In 1901, Young started 41 games. He won 31 of them. In 1903, Young helped Boston win the first World Series.

The team became known as the Red Sox in 1908. By that time, **Tris Speaker** had joined the team. Speaker was an outstanding center fielder. Other players marveled at his ability to track the ball. Speaker also gave opposing fielders trouble. He recorded a batting average of .337 in his nine years with Boston.

Speaker led Boston to World Series titles in 1912 and 1915. However, he left the team after the 1915 season. Fortunately for Boston fans, right fielder **Harry Hooper** picked up where Speaker left off. He helped the Red Sox win two more titles in 1916 and 1918.

Boston's championship days had passed by the 1930s. But the team was still loaded with stars like shortstop **Joe Cronin**. Cronin could hit for power. He also played great defense.

Two of the team's best players of all

THE BABE

Legendary slugger **Babe Ruth** started his career in Boston. Ruth was a pitcher at the time. "The Bambino" won more than 20 games twice in the 1910s. But after the 1919 season, the Sox sold Ruth to the New York Yankees. Boston didn't win another World Series for decades. Fans called it the Curse of the Bambino.

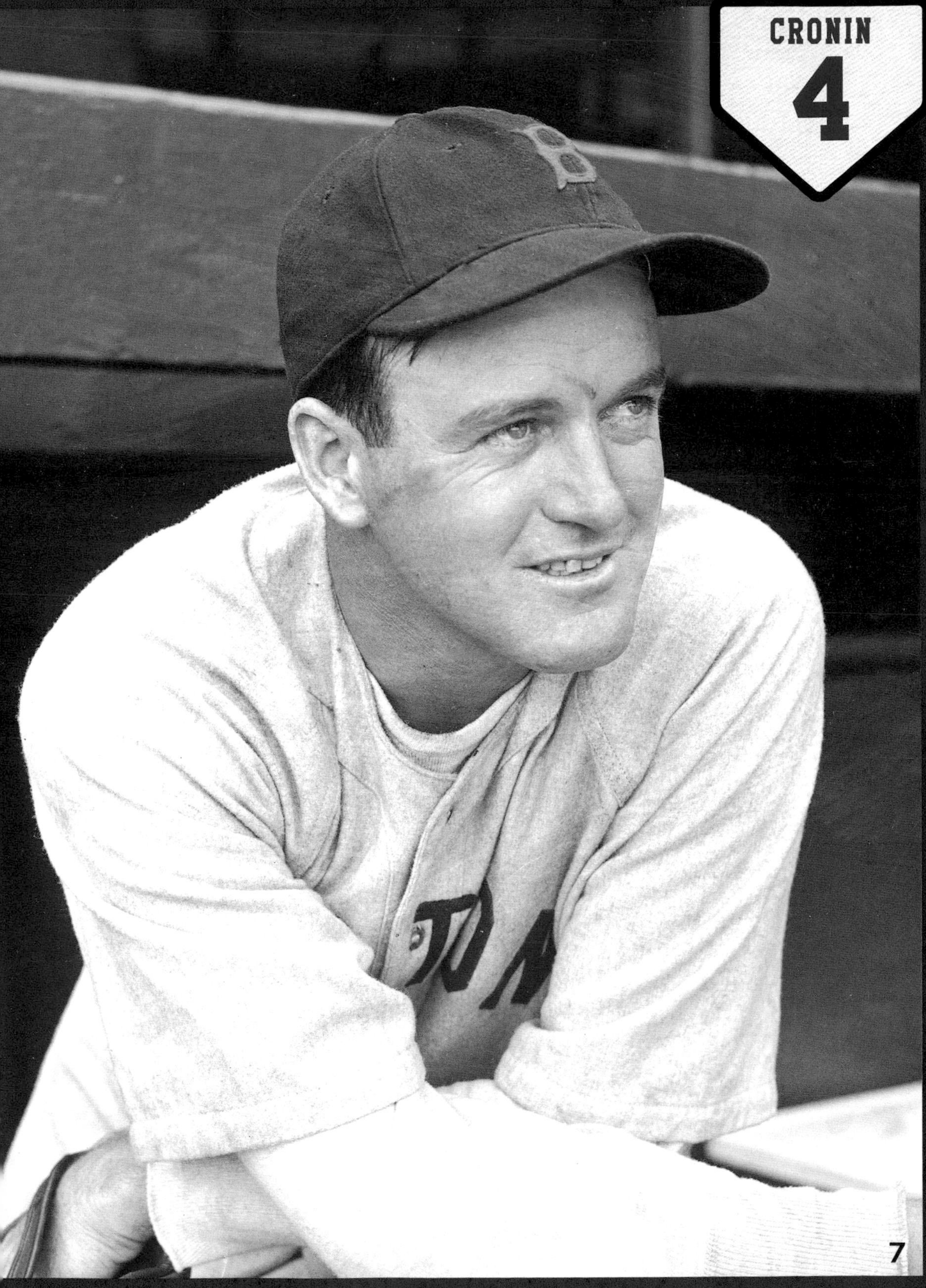
CRONIN
4

WILLIAMS
9

8

time arrived in the late 1930s. Second baseman **Bobby Doerr** was one of the top infielders in the game. Doerr made very few errors. He also had excellent power at the plate.

Few Red Sox measure up to left fielder **Ted Williams**. Williams was one of the greatest hitters in baseball history. In 1941, he had an incredible .406 batting average. Williams won six batting titles. He also earned two Most Valuable Player (MVP) Awards. Williams's career numbers could have been even better. However, he spent five years serving in the military.

STAT SPOTLIGHT

CAREER HOME RUNS
RED SOX TEAM RECORD
Ted Williams: 521

FISK
27

CHAPTER 2
NEW LEGENDS

Ted Williams left after the 1960 season. **Carl Yastrzemski** had big shoes to fill in left field. But "Yaz" more than held his own. He broke several of Ted Williams's records. Yaz played 23 seasons in Boston. When he retired, he was the only player in American League (AL) history with 3,000 hits and 400 homers.

Carlton Fisk hit home runs like no catcher before him. One of those blasts was extra special. Fisk hit the game-winning home run in Game 6 of the 1975 World Series. At first, it looked like it would be a foul ball. But Fisk waved his arms, hoping the ball would stay fair.

RICE
14

It became one of the most famous moments in baseball history.

After Yaz came **Jim Rice**. He was the third Hall of Famer to play left field in Boston. Rice had huge power. He hit 20 or more homers in 11 seasons. Rice could also hit the ball to all parts of the field. That kept fielders guessing.

Right fielder **Dwight Evans** spent 19 years in Boston. During that time, he won eight Gold Glove Awards. Evans was also a great all-around hitter for many years. Only Yaz played more games in a Red Sox uniform.

Luis Tiant did more than just pitch. He put on a show. Tiant's unusual pitching motion was fun to watch. It also made him hard to hit. Tiant had a positive impact in the locker room as well. Teammates loved his happy personality.

TOM YAWKEY

For many years, the street that runs past Fenway Park was called Yawkey Way. It was named after former Red Sox owner **Tom Yawkey**. He bought the team in 1933. He remained the owner until his death in 1976.

CLEMENS
21

Pitcher **Roger Clemens** was known for his power. He earned the nickname "Rocket" for his amazing fastball. During his 13 years with Boston, Clemens won three Cy Young Awards. He also won the MVP Award in 1986. That season, Clemens helped the Sox reach the World Series. However, Boston lost a heartbreaker to the New York Mets.

Third baseman **Wade Boggs** also played on that 1986 team. Boggs was an excellent contact hitter. He hit .368 in 1985. That was the best batting average for a Red Sox player since Ted Williams.

CAREER STRIKEOUTS
RED SOX TEAM RECORD
Roger Clemens: 2,590

GARCIAPARRA
5

CHAPTER 3
CURSE BREAKERS

Nomar Garciaparra quickly became the best Red Sox shortstop since Joe Cronin. Garciaparra was one of the top hitters in the game. He led the AL in batting average in both 1999 and 2000. During his nine seasons with Boston, Garciaparra made five All-Star teams. But Garciaparra was traded during the 2004 season. That meant he missed out on history.

The Red Sox hadn't won the World Series since 1918. The team was said to have been cursed for selling Babe Ruth. But the 2004 team seemed prepared to break that curse.

Jason Varitek was more than Boston's catcher. He was the team's captain. His great defense earned him three All-Star Game appearances. But he was best known as the leader of this era of Red Sox teams.

The Sox traded for **Pedro Martinez** right after he won the 1997 Cy Young Award. He went on to win two more before his final season in Boston in 2004. Martinez had a brilliant fastball and changeup combo. It kept hitters off-balance.

In left field was **Manny Ramirez**. The slugger was at his best in the postseason. He cranked out 29 postseason homers during his career. That was more than any other player in baseball history.

Ramirez formed a powerful duo with designated hitter

THE STEAL

Boston faced the New York Yankees in the 2004 American League Championship Series. The Red Sox trailed the Yankees three games to none. And in Game 4, Boston was down 4–3. However, in the bottom of the ninth, **Dave Roberts** stole second base. On the next pitch, a single to center field sent Roberts home. The Red Sox went on to win the game. Even more amazing, Boston rallied to win the series.

ORTIZ
34

David Ortiz. "Big Papi" had some of the
biggest hits in Red Sox history. He crushed
a three-run home run in Game 1 of the 2004

World Series. The Red Sox went on to finally break the curse.

Second baseman **Dustin Pedroia** debuted in 2006. He served as Boston's second baseman for the next 11 years. Pedroia was a great contact hitter and infielder. He also had some power despite being just 5-foot-9.

Midway through Pedroia's career, shortstop **Xander Bogaerts** joined the infield. Bogaerts quickly became one of the best shortstops in baseball. He helped Boston win the World Series in 2013 and 2018. Fans hoped that was just the beginning of another golden era.

TIMELINE

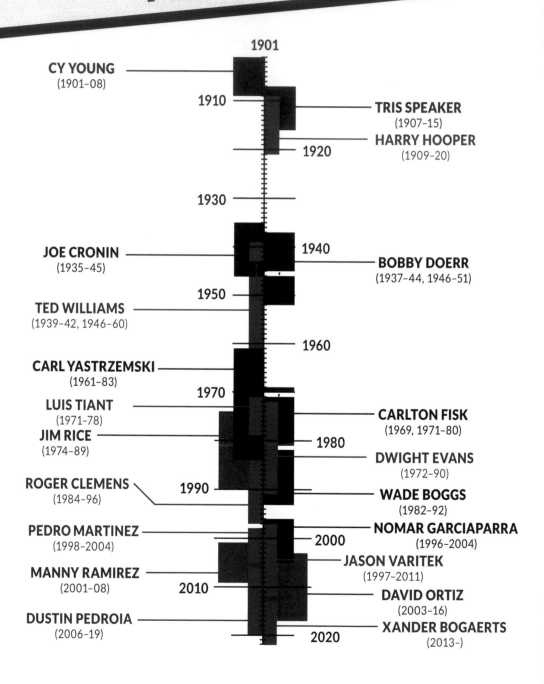

1901

CY YOUNG
(1901–08)

1910

TRIS SPEAKER
(1907–15)

HARRY HOOPER
(1909–20)

1920

1930

JOE CRONIN
(1935–45)

1940

BOBBY DOERR
(1937–44, 1946–51)

1950

TED WILLIAMS
(1939–42, 1946–60)

1960

CARL YASTRZEMSKI
(1961–83)

1970

LUIS TIANT
(1971–78)

CARLTON FISK
(1969, 1971–80)

JIM RICE
(1974–89)

1980

DWIGHT EVANS
(1972–90)

ROGER CLEMENS
(1984–96)

1990

WADE BOGGS
(1982–92)

PEDRO MARTINEZ
(1998–2004)

NOMAR GARCIAPARRA
(1996–2004)

2000

JASON VARITEK
(1997–2011)

MANNY RAMIREZ
(2001–08)

2010

DAVID ORTIZ
(2003–16)

DUSTIN PEDROIA
(2006–19)

XANDER BOGAERTS
(2013–)

2020

BOSTON RED SOX

Team history: Boston Americans (1901–07), Boston Red Sox (1908–)

World Series titles: 9 (1903, 1912, 1915, 1916, 1918, 2004, 2007, 2013, 2018)*

Key managers:

Joe Cronin (1935–47)
1,071-916-20 (.539)

Terry Francona (2004–11)
744-552 (.574), 2 World Series titles

MORE INFORMATION

To learn more about the Boston Red Sox, go to **pressboxbooks.com/AllAccess.**

These links are routinely monitored and updated to provide the most current information available.

*through 2021

GLOSSARY

captain
A team's leader.

changeup
A slow pitch that is meant to fool the batter into swinging too early.

debut
To make a first appearance.

era
A period of time in history.

fastball
A pitch thrown at a pitcher's top speed.

Gold Glove
An award that recognizes the top fielder in the league at each position.

postseason
A set of games to decide a league's champion.

slugger
A batter known for hitting home runs.

INDEX